M000266410

TABLE OF CONTENTS

Novel-Ties® are printed on recycled paper.

Copyright © 2007, 2018 by LEARNING LINKS

For the Teacher

This reproducible study guide to use in conjunction with the novel *Al Capone Does My Shirts* consists of lessons for guided reading. Written in chapter-by-chapter format, the guide contains a synopsis, pre-reading activities, vocabulary and comprehension exercises, as well as extension activities to be used as follow-up to the novel.

In a homogeneous classroom, whole class instruction with one title is appropriate. In a heterogeneous classroom, reading groups should be formed: each group works on a different novel at its own reading level. Depending upon the length of time devoted to reading in the classroom, each novel, with its guide and accompanying lessons, may be completed in three to six weeks.

Begin using NOVEL-TIES for reading development by distributing the novel and a folder to each child. Distribute duplicated pages of the study guide for students to place in their folders. After examining the cover and glancing through the book, students can participate in several pre-reading activities. Vocabulary questions should be considered prior to reading a chapter; all other work should be done after the chapter has been read. Comprehension questions can be answered orally or in writing. The classroom teacher should determine the amount of work to be assigned, always keeping in mind that readers must be nurtured and that the ultimate goal is encouraging students' love of reading.

The benefits of using NOVEL-TIES are numerous. Students read good literature in the original, rather than in abridged or edited form. The good reading habits, formed by practice in focusing on interpretive comprehension and literary techniques, will be transferred to the books students read independently. Passive readers become active, avid readers.

SYNOPSIS

On January 4, 1935, in the middle of the Great Depression, twelve-year-old Moose Flanagan and his family move to Alcatraz Island, where his father is to work as an electrician and a guard. Mrs. Flanagan hopes that her autistic daughter Natalie will be able to attend the Esther P. Marinoff School for challenged children in San Francisco. Although Natalie is actually fifteen years old, her mother claims she is ten so that her disability will seem less profound. Devoting herself to her daughter, Mrs. Flanagan sometimes neglects the needs of her son, a responsible young man who tries his best to support his sister and his family.

Homesick for his friends and his old baseball team, Moose is apprehensive about living on a prison island. To make matters worse, the warden's bossy and outspoken daughter, Piper, lures him into her schemes, such as selling the laundry services of Alcatraz convicts to her classmates. To do so, she talks up the fact that the notorious gangster Al Capone is imprisoned on Alcatraz, even though this goes against one of her father's rules. Afraid to displease Piper, Moose and the other children on the island aid in her scheme and ultimately get into trouble with the warden.

When Natalie's bad behavior causes her to be rejected from the Esther P. Marinoff school, Mrs. Flanagan hires Carrie Kelly to prepare Natalie to enter the school. To pay for this new expense, Moose's mother gives piano lessons. Now it is up to Moose to take care of Natalie after school, dealing with her tantrums and constant needs. His mother challenges Moose to introduce Natalie to other children on the island, allowing her to lead as normal a life as possible. This new responsibility causes Moose to lose his chance to play baseball on a team organized by his new friend Scout.

Although all this is upsetting to Moose, he does begin to notice a change in Natalie. She is becoming more a part of the group of children and less difficult to handle. Moose takes her with him to obtain a baseball for Scout that was hit beyond the yard from one of the convicts' games. Sometimes, he leaves Natalie alone playing with her button collection, as he goes off on his own. One day he returns to find Natalie happily talking to a convict, number 105. Horrified, Moose drags his sister home. He later confronts his mother about Natalie's true age and the danger of having a convict notice her, but he does not mention convict 105, afraid that his failure to protect his sister will disappoint his father.

The relationship between Moose and his mother becomes strained when Moose refuses to take his sister outside, afraid of Natalie's acquaintance with the convict. After throwing a terrible tantrum, Natalie demands to go outside, a request he feels he cannot deny. The day before Natalie's interview for the Esther P. Marinoff School, Moose once again takes her out to calm her. Once outside, she runs to convict 105 to say goodbye, Moose and Piper watch as Natalie holds hands with the man, just like a normal girl of her age.

When Mrs. Flanagan has a tenth birthday party for her sixteen-year-old daughter, Piper suggests that everyone knows Natalie is much older than ten. Moose stands up to his mother, declaring that lying about Natalie's age will ruin any chances she has. Mrs. Flanagan is furious until she realizes that Moose just wants what is best for his sister.

Despite a good interview, Natalie is rejected once again from the Esther P. Marinoff School. Moose, who now sees the school as his sister's only chance, goes to the warden to beg him to use his influence to get Natalie enrolled there. He angers the warden, however, when he suggests asking Al Capone to help in the endeavor. Undeterred, Moose writes a letter to Capone and with Piper's help gets it into the pile of censored letters on their way to the prisoners. When the school year ends, Moose receives the great news that Natalie has been accepted to a new branch of the Esther P. Marinoff School, one for older students. In his shirt, which has just come back from the Alcatraz laundry, Moose finds a note that simply says "Done."

BACKGROUND INFORMATION

San Francisco

The city of San Francisco is located on the tip of the San Francisco Peninsula in Northern California. The city is famous for its forty-three hills, all of which are within city limits. Several islands are a part of the city, including Alcatraz Island and Treasure Island.

On the morning of April 18, 1906, a major earthquake struck San Francisco, destroying about three-quarters of the city. The citizens quickly rebuilt, however, celebrating the rebirth of their city at the Panama-Pacific International Exposition in 1915. In the years that followed, San Francisco established itself as a financial center. When the stock market crashed in 1929, not a single city-based bank failed. In fact, it was during the Great Depression that the city began two great engineering projects—the building of the San Francisco-Oakland Bay Bridge and the Golden Gate Bridge. It was also in this period, in August 1934, that the island of Alcatraz, a former military stockade, became a federal prison. During its twenty-nine years as a prison, the jail housed such notorious figures as Machine Gun Kelly, Robert Franklin Stroud (the Birdman of Alcatraz), and Al Capone. The facility also housed the prison staff and their families.

Al Capone

Alphonse Capone, better known as Al Capone or Scarface, was an infamous gangster who ruled over Chicago's organized crime during the second half of the 1920s. Born in Brooklyn, New York, in 1899 to two Italian immigrants, young Al never responded well to authority. Facing a life of low-paying jobs, he joined a street gang and began a life of crime.

After moving to Chicago to avoid a murder charge, Capone eventually became the head of Chicago's crime families. With his mob at its prime, Capone bought off city officials and virtually ran the streets of Chicago. On February 14, 1929 he ordered the shooting of Bugs Moran, a rival gangster. In what is known as the St. Valentine's Day Massacre, Capone's men killed a group of seven people, but Moran was not in the group. The much-publicized event prompted law officials to renew efforts to tackle the problem of organized crime.

Unable to convict Capone on any mob-related criminal acts, the federal government began looking at other ways to convict him. The Internal Revenue Service gathered tax evasion information on Capone. On November 24, 1929, Capone was sentenced to eleven years in Federal prison for tax evasion. He was jailed at Alcatraz from 1934 to 1939. Capone's health was never the same after leaving jail. He died of a stroke and pneumonia on January 25, 1947.

Autism

Autism is a developmental disorder that affects brain functions. It is characterized by poor development of communication skills, social skills, and reasoning. Children may appear normal until almost three years old, although some show signs of autism younger than a year of age. Symptoms include lack of eye contact, obsessive behavior, failure to communicate with words, violent tantrums, and repetitive movements such as rocking. Those with autism may not respond to people or may focus on one object for long periods of time. They often doggedly stick to certain routines and rituals, becoming very upset when these patterned behaviors are changed. When autistic people do speak, they usually refer to themselves by name instead of using the pronouns "I" or "me."

Some people with autism, called autistic savants, have extraordinary skills not exhibited by most persons. There are many forms of savant abilities. The most common forms involve mathematical calculations, memory feats, artistic abilities, and musical abilities. A mathematical ability which some autistic individuals display is calendar memory. If you give them a month, day, and year, they will tell you what day of the week it was. Others can multiply and divide large numbers in their head with little or no hesitation.

PRE-READING QUESTIONS AND ACTIVITIES

1. Preview the book by reading the title and the author's name and by looking at the picture on the cover. What do you think the book is about? Will it be serious or humorous? When and where do you think it takes place?

2. Read the Background Information about the city of San Francisco, Alcatraz, and Al Capone on page three of this study guide. Then read the Author's Note at the back of the novel to find out more information. Make a list of any questions you have about the material. Then, as you read the novel, see if you can find the answers to these questions.

3. **Cooperative Learning Activity:** Learn about autism in the Background Information on page four in this study guide and the Author's Note at the back of the novel. Do some additional research on the topic. Then brainstorm with a small group of classmates to fill in the first two columns of a K-W-L chart, such as the one below. When you finish the book, return to the chart to complete the third column.

Autism

What I Know –K–	What I Want to Learn –W–	What I Learned –L–

4. Imagine that you have a brother or sister with autism. What increased responsibilities might you have? How might this affect your everyday life? How would you feel about this? As you read the novel, compare your feelings with those of Moose.

5. Have you read any other books set in the United States in the 1930s? If so, when and where were these stories set? What types of problems did people in these books have to face?

6. As you read, use the diagram of Alcatraz Island at the beginning of the book to trace the action of the story.

7. **Cooperative Learning Activity:** Work with a small cooperative learning group to discuss the meaning of "responsibility." Make a list of the responsibilities you owe your family. Then make a list of the responsibilities you owe yourself. Do any of these conflict? What problems might this conflict cause?

8. *Al Capone Does My Shirts* is a book of historical fiction—one that uses history as a background for imagined events. The characters in such a work may be fictional or historical or both. Discuss with your classmates other works of historical fiction they have read and the periods of history they covered. What do they enjoy about this type of book? What challenges does an author face when writing such a work?

9. With your classmates read the first three paragraphs of the story and respond to the following questions:
   - What do you learn about the character telling the story?
   - Where does the story take place?
   - How does the author grab the reader's attention?
   - What do you want to find out?

Pre-Reading Questions and Activities (cont.)

10. Respond to the statements in the following Anticipation Guide by placing a check [✔] next to each statement with which you agree in the "You" column. After you read the book, place a check in the "Author" column next to each item with which the author agrees.

	You	Author
1. Children with severe autism should remain at home with their families.		
2. Children with severe autism do best when boarding at a school with other children who have similar problems.		
3. Living with a special needs child makes a family unit stronger.		
4. Caring for a special needs child at home can tear a family apart.		
5. Everyone in a family needs to make sacrifices for a child with special needs.		
6. When there is a handicapped child in a family, that child should receive most of the parents' attention.		
7. The normal child in a family where there is a handicapped child will often be neglected.		
8. It is difficult for a new student at school to make friends.		
9. When faced with choices in life, there is only one that is right and others that are wrong.		
10. Sometimes it is necessary to do something wrong in order to reach a worthwhile goal.		
11. A lie is always wrong.		

CHAPTERS 1 – 5

Vocabulary: Draw a line from each word on the left to its definition on the right. Then use the numbered words to fill in the blanks in the sentences below.

1. convicted   a. separate sections

2. affliction   b. fits of bad temper

3. tantrums   c. place for the care of a large group of helpless people

4. evasion   d. found guilty

5. compartments   e. getting away with something by trickery

6. obedient   f. cause of suffering or trouble

7. asylum   g. kind, gentle, and showing mercy

8. humane   h. following orders

. . . .

1. In the past, orphans and the mentally ill were sent to live in a(n) _____.

2. My refrigerator has separate _____ for fruits, vegetables, eggs, and cheese.

3. Troubled by the way prisoners were treated, my mother organized a letter-writing campaign to promote more _____ treatment.

4. Mental illness is often left untreated as it can be an invisible _____.

5. The _____ bank robber was on his way to prison.

6. The _____ dog came running over when its master called.

7. Little children sometimes have _____ when they do not get what they want.

8. Watching television instead of doing my homework assignments is a clear _____ of my responsibilities.

> Read to find out how Moose feels about his new home at Alcatraz.

Chapters 1 – 5 (cont.)

Questions:

1. Why does the Flanagan family come to live on Alcatraz Island?

2. How does Moose sleep on his first night on Alcatraz? Why does he do this?

3. Why does Mrs. Flanagan celebrate Natalie's tenth birthday each year?

4. Why does Piper come unexpectedly to Moose's house on the Flanagans' first day on Alcatraz Island?

5. Why is Moose angered by Piper at their first meeting?

6. What evidence shows that Natalie feels that Moose is important in her life?

7. How does Moose feel after the family leaves Natalie at the school?

Questions for Discussion:

1. Do you think that Mr. and Mrs. Flanagan are justified in moving to Alcatraz? Is it fair to Moose?

2. Do you think that Moose should be asked to babysit for his sister Natalie?

3. In your opinion, which of Moose's parents has a better understanding of him?

4. Do you think Moose resents his sister? Would he be justified in feeling this way?

5. Do you think Natalie will have a successful experience at her new school?

Literary Element: Setting

In literature, the setting refers to the time and place in which the story occurs. Setting is especially important in a historical novel such as this one.

What is the setting of this novel?

_____

What details about the setting make the characters' times and lifestyles seem real?

_____

_____

Chapters 1 – 5 (cont.)

Literary Devices:

I. *Point of View* — Point of view in literature refers to the person telling the story. When one of the characters acts as the narrator, this is called the first-person point of view. When the author as an outside observer tells the story, it is called a third-person point of view.

From whose point of view is this story told?

_____

List three statements the narrator makes about himself that help you to understand his character. What does each statement reveal about him?

_____

_____

_____

_____

II. *Simile* — A simile is a figure of speech in which two unlike objects are compared using the words "like" or "as." For example:

A haze rises from the bay like a wall of gray closing me off from everything.

What is being compared in this simile?

_____

What is the effect of this comparison?

_____

_____

III. *Metaphor* — A metaphor is a figure of speech in which a comparison between two unlike objects is suggested or implied. For example:

I hate being the brother of a stone.

What is being compared?

_____

What does this help reveal Moose's feelings about his sister's condition?

_____

_____

Chapters 1 – 5 (cont.)

In some metaphors the comparison is extended for a few sentences. What is life being compared to in the following extended metaphor?

> "Nobody knows how things will turn out, that's why they go ahead and play the game, Moose. You give it your all and sometimes amazing things happen, but it's hardly ever what you expect."

_____

_____

Why is this an apt comparison?

_____

_____

Writing Activity:

Imagine you are Piper. In a journal entry, tell about your first meeting with Moose, giving your impressions of the new boy.

CHAPTERS 6 – 10

Vocabulary: Synonyms are words with similar meanings. Draw a line from each word in column A to its synonym in column B. Then use the words in column A to fill in the blanks in the sentences below.

	A			B	
1.	heinous		a.	mocking
2.	incredibly		b.	corrective
3.	hordes		c.	carefully
4.	contraption		d.	unbelievably
5.	deliberately		e.	evil
6.	remedial		f.	beaming
7.	sarcastic		g.	device
8.	radiant		h.	crowds

. . . .

1. Because he has trouble reading, Jeff attends a(n) _____ reading class.

2. The day of the super sale, _____ of people were waiting outside to get into the store.

3. After winning the spelling bee, the girl flashed a(n) _____ smile at her family and the audience.

4. People who commit _____ crimes should be sent to prison for a long time.

5. "Don't rush!" was my brother's _____ comment as I slowy put on my clothes.

6. The hurricane was very powerful, but _____ nobody was injured.

7. Maya _____ put the finishing touches on her science project.

8. Jack built a(n) _____ to scare rabbits out of the garden.

Chapters 6 – 10 (cont.)

Read to find out if life improves for Moose on Alcatraz.

Questions:

1. Why does the warden call Moose into his office?

2. Why doesn't the warden want anyone to talk about the inmate Al Capone or life on Alcatraz Island?

3. Why does Moose feel self-conscious when he walks into his classroom?

4. Which one of her father's rules does Piper break in Miss Bimp's class?

5. Why does Moose change the outline for his oral report?

6. Why is Moose reluctant to help Piper with her project?

7. How does playing baseball make Moose feel better about living on Alcatraz?

8. How do some of the children manage to get balls from the convicts' games?

9. Why does Annie tell Moose that he must get along with Piper?

0. Why does Mr. Purdy call the Flanagans?

Questions for Discussion:

1. Do you think it was really necessary for the warden to call Moose into his office? Do you think the five rules make sense?

2. How do you think Piper took advantage of Moose while she sat in on his meeting with her father?

3. Do you agree with Moose that life for him on Alcatraz is like a prison in many ways?

4. Do you think Moose will ultimately help Piper with her laundry scheme?

5. Why do you think Moose gives Mr. Purdy's news to his father and not his mother?

Social Studies Connection:

Piper compares Moose to Babe Ruth. Do some research to find out about this famous baseball player. Why does Moose take the comparison as a compliment?

Chapters 6 – 10 (cont.)

Literary Element: Characterization

Characters in literature are revealed by what they say and do and by what others say about them. In a chart, such as the one below, list important information you have learned about some of the characters in the book. Continue to fill in the chart as you read. You may also add characters to the chart.

Character	Physical Appearance	Personality Traits
Moose		
Piper		
Mrs. Flanagan		
Mr. Flanagan		

Literary Device: Simile

For each of the following similes, tell what is being compared. Then indicate the emotion that Moose feels.

My voice squeaks high like a rodent's.

_____

_____

My ears are like two heaters attached to my head.

_____

_____

The ball, my glove, my arm are all working together like greased motor parts.

_____

_____

Writing Activities:

1. Imagine that you write an advice column. Moose has written to you for advice on how to handle Piper. Write a column advising him what to do.

2. Write about a time when you moved to a new place or were in a situation where you had to make new friends. How did you feel? What did you do to help you fit in?

CHAPTERS 11 – 15

Vocabulary: Use the words from the Word Box and the clues below to complete the crossword puzzle.

WORD BOX
adjustment
cultivated
diagnosis
facility
frustrating
mercilessly
miraculously
natters
notorious
replicate
residential
revving
skirmish
unresponsive
wheedle

Across

1. not reacting right away
4. room or building that provides a special service
6. cruelly
8. process of becoming used to
10. talks on at length
12. increasing the speed of an engine
13. amazingly

Down

2. containing homes
3. copy or repeat
4. annoying and trying
5. identification of a disease by studying the symptoms
7. improved by studying or training
9. coax
10. well-known, especially because of something bad
11. minor fight

Chapters 11 – 15 (cont.)

> Read to find out why Natalie must leave the Esther P. Marinoff School.

Questions:

1. How does Mrs. Flanagan react when she receives the news that Natalie must leave school?

2. Why is Moose both proud of his mother and angry at her at the meeting with Mr. Purdy?

3. Why does Mr. Purdy feel that Natalie is not ready for his school?

4. Why does Moose finally agree to help Piper with her laundry project?

5. Why does Moose become angry at his mother?

6. How does Moose get Natalie to put on her blue dress?

7. Why is Moose happy that Natalie is with him when they go to watch the convicts march up to the cell house?

Questions for Discussion:

1. Do you think Mr. Purdy is justified in requiring Natalie to leave his school?

2. Do you think that Mrs. Flanagan should require Moose to watch Natalie and possibly give up his baseball game?

3. Why do you think that Moose prefers to play things safe and not break the rules?

4. Do you think that Mrs. Kelly's strategies for improving Natalie's behavior will work?

5. Why do you think Piper's classmates were anxious to go along with the laundry scheme?

Writing Activity:

Think about a time when you were tempted to break the rules. What were the circumstances? Did you break the rules or not? What was the outcome? Looking back, would you have done anything differently?

Chapters 11 – 15 (cont.)

Literary Element: Conflict

A conflict is a struggle between opposing forces. An external conflict is a character's struggle against an outside force, such as nature, society, or another person. An internal conflict is a personal struggle that takes place within a character's mind. In the chart below, list the conflicts that have occurred in the story so far. Indicate how some of these problems have been resolved. As you continue the story, add to the chart.

External Conflicts	**Resolutions**
Internal Conflicts	**Resolutions**

CHAPTERS 16 – 20

Vocabulary: Ue a word from the Word Box to replace each underlined word or phrase in the following sentences. Write the word on the line below the sentence.

WORD BOX			
culpability	indignity	procuring	shenanigans
elaborate	preposterous	quavering	unseemly

1. The children felt more comfortable eating in the kitchen than eating in the <u>overly decorated</u> dining room.

    _____

2. It is <u>absurd</u> to eat peas with a knife.

    _____

3. She felt it was an <u>insult</u> to receive her invitation to the party long after everyone else.

    _____

4. The mother told her children to stop their <u>mischievous pranks</u> or they would be punished.

    _____

5. It is usually <u>not proper</u> to laugh or have loud conversations in a courtroom.

    _____

6. The children had to share <u>responsibility for wrongdoing</u> for the prank.

    _____

7. My brother's voice was <u>shaking</u> as he told me the bad news.

    _____

8. Our team works together in <u>bringing about</u> a solution to any problem.

    _____

Read to learn how the warden reacts when he finds out about the laundry scheme.

Chapters 16 – 20 (cont.)

Questions:

1. Why are Piper's customers disappointed with their laundry?

2. Why does Scout become angry at Moose and bar him from playing baseball?

3. How does Natalie help the children when Piper needs to divide the laundry money?

4. How did the warden find out about Piper's laundry project?

5. How does the warden react when the other children tell him that the laundry project was Piper's idea?

6. Why does Natalie become quiet and rigid?

7. Why is Moose surprised when his father punishes him?

Questions for Discussion:

1. Do you think Scout should have been more understanding of Moose's problem?

2. In what ways has Natalie become part of the group of children? What advantages are there to this? What problems might it cause?

3. What do you think Piper whispers to her father as the other children leave the room? Do you agree with Moose that she will "get out of this"?

4. In what way does Moose share the responsibility for the laundry scheme? Do you think his punishment is fair?

5. Do you think the anger that Moose's father shows is justified? Why won't he allow his son to tell him the entire story?

6. Why do you think Mrs. Flanagan becomes angry and upset when she sees the other children gathered around Natalie?

Science Connection:

There are eucalyptus trees on Alcatraz Island. Do some research to find out about these trees. What do they look like? Where do they originally come from? When and how were they first introduced to California? What advantages have they been to the state? What problems have they caused?

Social Studies Connection:

Del's mother threatens to write a letter to the *San Francisco Chronicle*. Find out more about this newspaper. When was it founded and by whom? How did it get to be the city's largest newspaper? What prizes has it received? How is the paper different today from the way it was ten years ago?

Chapters 16 – 20 (cont.)

Literary Devices:

I. *Personification*—Personification is a literary device in which an author grants human qualities to inanimate objects. For example:

> The silence presses down on me.

What is being personified?

_____

What mood does this convey? How does this help convey the mood?

_____

_____

Here is another example of personification:

> The words crawl out of my throat.

What is being personified?

_____

What does this help reveal about Moose?

_____

_____

II. *Symbolism*—A symbol in literature is an object, event, or character that represents an idea or a set of ideas. What do you think baseball represents for Moose? What do the buttons represent for Natalie? In what way are these two symbols similar?

_____

_____

_____

_____

Writing Activities:

1. Imagine you are Mrs. Flanagan. In a journal entry, write about the argument you had with Moose over baseball. How did you feel about the situation? Why did you react the way you did?

2. After losing Scout as a friend, Moose writes a letter to Pete. Imagine you are Moose and write that letter.

CHAPTERS 21 – 26

Vocabulary: Use the context to determine the meaning of the underlined word in each of the following sentences. Then compare your definition to a dictionary definition.

1. Those rude remarks would be an <u>offense</u> to anyone.
   Your definition_____

   Dictionary definition _____

2. Being very <u>possessive</u> of his toys, the child does not like to share them with others.
   Your definition_____

   Dictionary definition _____

3. She could not stand the <u>humiliation</u> when her friends laughed at her painting.
   Your definition_____

   Dictionary definition _____

4. Eager to get home before it began to rain, I quickened my <u>pace</u>.
   Your definition_____

   Dictionary definition _____

5. When heavy rains <u>eroded</u> the hillside, our house was in danger of toppling over.
   Your definition_____

   Dictionary definition _____

6. After years of research, the scientist is on the <u>verge</u> of making a major discovery.
   Your definition_____

   Dictionary definition _____

7. I like being on her team because she is a <u>diligent</u> worker.
   Your definition_____

   Dictionary definition _____

8. The toys were strewn <u>helter-skelter</u> in the living room, making it impossible to enter.
   Your definition_____

   Dictionary definition _____

Read to find out what Piper's next scheme will be.

Chapters 21 – 26 (cont.)

Questions:

1. How has Natalie behaved since she had a fit the day the children met with the warden?

2. Why does Piper want the children to be on the nine-thirty boat to the city on Sunday and return at ten?

3. In what way does Theresa act against Piper's wishes?

4. How does Piper try to get Mrs. Capone's attention? Why doesn't this work?

5. What does get Mrs. Capone's attention?

6. Why doesn't Mrs. Capone get to visit her son?

7. How do Moose and Scout become friends again?

8. Why is Moose pleased to hear Natalie's imitation of Mrs. Kelly?

9. What evidence reveals that Natalie has had more than one meeting with convict 105?

Questions for Discussion:

1. Why do you think that Natalie seems to be improving?

2. Why do you think Mrs. Capone does not pay attention to Piper?

3. Why do you think that Mrs. Capone's face lights up when she cares for Rocky?

4. Why do you think that Moose is troubled when he learns that Scout has become friendly with Piper?

5. In your opinion, why is it important to Moose that he find a ball for Scout?

6. Do you think that Moose overreacts when he sees Natalie with convict 105? Why do you think he acts this way?

Social Studies Connection:

Moose learns about the Louisiana Purchase in school. Do some research to find out what lands were acquired by this purchase and why this was significant.

Literary Devices:

I. *Metaphor*—What is being compared in the following passage?

    A gap in the fence is a magnet.

_____

What does this explain?

_____

_____

Chapters 21 – 26 (cont.)

II. *Cliffhanger*—A cliffhanger in literature is a device borrowed from silent, serialized films in which an episode ends at a suspenseful moment. In a book it usually appears at the end of a chapter to encourage the reader to continue on in the book. What is the cliffhanger at the end of Chapter Twenty-three?

_____

_____

What is the cliffhanger at the end of Chapter Twenty-five?

_____

_____

III. *Simile*—What is being compared in this passage?

> The con jumps and Natalie's smile, like some kind of rare bird sighting, slips away.

_____

What is the effect of this comparison?

_____

_____

Writing Activity:

The convict obviously finds out about Moose from Natalie. What else could they have been talking about? Write the conversation you think the two had just before Moose arrives.

CHAPTERS 27 – 32

Vocabulary: Antonyms are words with opposite meanings. Draw a line from each word in column A to its antonym in column B. Then use the words in column A to fill in the blanks in the sentences below.

A	B
1. selective	a. fall
2. jeopardize	b. attract
3. disloyal	c. protect
4. hover	d. delicate
5. repel	e. haphazard
6. forlorn	f. happy
7. strapping	g. faithful

. . . .

1. My sister became _____ when her best friend moved to a town far away.

2. Birds will _____ over their nests to keep an eye on their young.

3. My brother spent hours shopping in the book store because he is very _____ about what he reads.

4. A forest fire will _____ the animal life in the area.

5. Ted is a _____ young man, nothing like his frail brother.

6. The like poles of two magnets _____ each other.

7. It is _____ to say bad things about your friends behind their backs.

> Read to find out what Moose tells his parents about Natalie and convict 105.

Questions:

1. Why is Moose uncharacteristically rough with Natalie as they walk home?

2. Why does Moose slam the door in ~~Natalie's~~ Piper's face?

3. Why is Piper excited about Natalie's relationship with convict 105?

Chapters 27 – 32 (cont.)

4. Why does Moose confront his mother about Natalie's age?

5. Why is Moose's mother angry at her son for no longer taking Natalie outside?

6. Why does Mrs. Flanagan take Natalie's buttons away from her? How does Natalie react?

7. Why does Moose finally take Natalie outside?

8. Why does Moose ask his father whether he is responsible for Natalie's behavior? How does he respond?

Questions for Discussion:

1. Why do you think Moose's mother and father hold on to their optimistic expectations for Natalie?

2. Do you think Moose should have revealed to his parents the whole story about Natalie and convict 105, instead of telling them only part of the story?

3. Do you think Moose should trust any part of Piper's plan for Natalie?

4. Do you think that Moose will continue to have so much responsibility for his sister?

2. In your opinion, will Mrs. Flanagan be able to give her son more attention in order to better understand his needs?

Literary Devices:

I. *Simile* — Tell what is being compared in each of the following similes. Then indicate how each helps convey Moose's feeling about his mother.

> Her [Mrs. Flanagan's] eyes are like teeth tearing into me.

_____

_____

> We both keep our space, never passing close to one
> another, like magnets set to repel.

_____

_____

Chapters 27 – 32 (cont.)

II. *Personification*—Tell what is being personified in each of the following examples. Then indicate how each example of personification helps the reader to visualize a scene or understand an emotion.

Her [Piper's] eyes are burrowing inside me now.

_____

_____

The air itself carries her [Mrs. Flanagan's] blame.

_____

_____

Writing Activities:
Imagine you are Mr. Flanagan. In a letter to Moose's grandmother, write about the problems between your wife and son, indicating your feelings about the situation.

CHAPTERS 33 – 36

Vocabulary: Word analogies are equations in which the first pair of words has the same relationship as the second pair of words. For example: TINY is to HUGE as EXCITING is to BORING. Both pairs of words are opposites. Choose the best word from the Word Box to complete each of the analogies below.

```
                        WORD BOX
        attitude     obsessed    seething    understatement
        obnoxious    rotation    teetering   vulnerable
```

1. CALM is to EXCITED as DISINTERESTED is to _____.

2. MERCY is to KINDNESS as _____ is to POSE.

3. HELPLESS is to _____ as PECULIAR is to STRANGE.

4. _____ is to PLEASANT as SIMPLE is to ELABORATE.

5. SUPPORTING is to ASSISTING as WOBBLING is to _____.

6. PICTURE is to PAINTING as _____ is to CIRCLING.

7. EXAGGERATION is to _____ as STRENGTH is to WEAKNESS.

8. _____ is to INSULT as PLEASED is to COMPLIMENT.

> Read to find out what happens on Natalie's birthday.

Questions:

1. Why is Mrs. Flanagan extremely nervous before Natalie's birthday?

2. Why doesn't Mrs. Flanagan choose to stay home the day before the interview?

3. According to Piper, why does she drop by the Flanagan's apartment?

4. Why won't Natalie follow Moose, as she usually does, when they go outside?

5. What conflicting emotions does Moose have as he watches Natalie with 105?

6. Why does Moose want his mother to be honest about Natalie's age?

7. Why is Mrs. Flanagan no longer angry with Moose?

8. Why does Mrs. Caconi come to the Flanagans' apartment?

Chapters 33 – 36 (cont.)

Questions for Discussion:

1. What behaviors does Natalie exhibit that suggest she is improving? On the other hand, what behaviors show that she remains the same?

2. Why do you think that Piper tags along when Natalie goes to meet 105? Is she a help or a hindrance to Moose?

3. Do you think that the children on Alcatraz behave toward Natalie in the way that Moose and his parents expected?

4. Why do you think Mr. Flanagan expresses pride in both of his children?

5. Why do you think Natalie has become friends with Theresa?

6. How do you think Mrs. Flanagan will react to Mrs. Caconi's news?

Literary Elements:

I. *Humor*—Humor in a story is the quality that makes you laugh aloud or smile. Even though this novel deals with some serious topics, Theresa provides humor throughout. Describe a situation where Theresa's actions or comments make you smile or laugh. Then tell why you found this situation funny.

_____

_____

_____

_____

II. *Mood*—Mood is the overall atmosphere or feeling of a literary work. Happiness or sadness, terror or tranquility—mood can be any strong feeling or emotion the author creates, often by using descriptive details. The author can convey different moods within a work, sometimes even within a single paragraph. Read the following passage:

> We walk up the steep road to Piper's house. It's beautiful out. The blue-black night all around, the black, black water. San Francisco like a bright box of lights. This is the most beautiful place I've ever been. Then I look at the cell house, sad and silent. The lights are dim. I don't hear anything except from deep inside the sound of one metal cup clanking the length of the bars and one lone voice calling for help.

What two contrasting moods are set by the passage?

_____

Underline once those words that create the first mood. Then underline twice those words that create the second mood.

Chapters 33 – 36 (cont.)

III. *Characterization*—Moose finds himself both attracted to Piper and appalled by her behavior. Use the Venn diagram below to compare Moose and Piper. In the overlapping part of the circles, write the qualities they have in common.

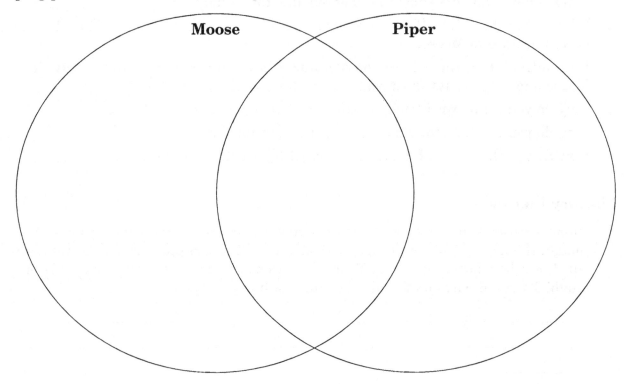

Writing Activities:

1. Do you think that Moose and Piper could ever be boyfriend and girlfriend? Using the information from the Venn diagram, write a few well-developed paragraphs supporting your opinion.

2. Imagine that you are Mr. Purdy. In a report to the school board, discuss why you feel that Natalie is still not ready to enroll in the Esther P. Marinoff School.

CHAPTERS 37 – 40

Vocabulary: Use the context to help you choose the best meaning for the underlined word or phrase in each of the following sentences. Circle the letter of the meaning you choose.

1. She asked her parents to <u>reconsider</u> letting her go to the party.

    a. forget about   b. not worry about   c. think again about   d. speak up about

2. The judge's decision will serve as a <u>precedent</u> in other courts.

    a. standard   b. mistake   c. problem   d. rumor

3. The owner's friends always receive <u>preferential</u> treatment at the restaurant.

    a. poor   b. distant   c. ordinary   d. special

4. The unfair trial was a <u>mockery</u> of justice.

    a. amusing case   b. good attempt   c. false imitation   d. fine example

5. Her loyal support of a friend in distress was <u>admirable</u>.

    a. worthy   b. foolish   c. shameful   d. peculiar

6. Letters from the battlefield <u>were censored</u> to make sure military information did not fall into enemy hands.

    a. were   b. had parts   c. were delivered   d. had parts
       broadcast   deleted   late   added
       in the media

7. Be sure to make a <u>duplicate</u> of your report just in case one gets lost.

    a. longer version b. exact copy   c. shorter version   d. illustrated copy

8. The excited crowd burst into <u>spontaneous</u> cheers at the skillful play.

    a. scornful   b. intended   c. halfhearted   d. unplanned

> Read to find out how Moose tries to help Natalie get into
> the Esther P. Marinoff School.

Chapters 37 – 40 (cont.)

Questions:

1. Why does Moose call Carrie Kelly?
2. Why does Warden Williams refuse to solicit Al Capone's help in getting Natalie into the Esther P. Marinoff School?
3. How does Mrs. Flanagan behave after learning that Natalie has not been accepted at the Esther P. Marinoff School?
4. How does Piper help Moose send a letter with a plea on Natalie's behalf to Al Capone?
5. Why are the warden, Natalie, and Moose's parents at the dock to meet the boat that is bringing the school children back from San Francisco?
6. What is strange about Mr. Purdy's sudden change of heart?

Questions for Discussion:

1. Why does Moose, who never wants to break rules, now want to break one of the warden's rules? Do you think he is justified to do so? Do you think the warden is justified in his refusal?
2. Why do you think Piper agrees to help Moose with his letter to Al Capone?
3. What does the word "done" inside his shirt suggest?
4. How do you think that Natalie really gets accepted to school?
5. Do you think that Natalie will be able to stay and progress this time at the Esther P. Marinoff School?

Literary Connection:

Piper asked Al Capone to check out *Jane Eyre* from the library, knowing no convict would read this book. Find out who wrote *Jane Eyre* and what it is about. If possible, read the first chapter. Why do you think male convicts would not be interested in this book?

Literary Elements:

I. *Theme*—An author usually writes a story to communicate a general message about life and how people behave. This message, or theme, can typically be stated in one sentence. A long literary work might have more than one theme. Compile a list of important themes in this book. Consider what the book is saying about the following topics:

- dealing with change
- personal strength and courage
- family
- friendship
- responsibility
- communication
- truth
- overcoming handicaps

Chapters 37 – 40 (cont.)

I. *Characterization* — During the course of a novel some characters evolve and grow while others remain the same. Tell whether or not each of the following characters has changed from the beginning of the novel. If you indicate that a character has grown, describe what changes have taken place.

1. Moose _____

_____

_____

2. Piper _____

_____

_____

3. Mrs. Flanagan _____

_____

_____

4. Mr. Flanagan _____

_____

_____

Writing Activities:

1. Piper admits saying she enjoyed staying at her grandmother's house to save face. Write about a time when you made up a story or stretched the truth to save face.

2. Imagine that you are Moose. Write a thank you letter to Al Capone for his help. Or if you prefer, write a letter to Mrs. Kelly expressing your gratitude for the work she has done with Natalie.

AL CAPONE DOES MY SHIRTS

CLOZE ACTIVITY

The following passage is taken from Chapter Twenty-six of the novel. Read it through completely. Then fill in each blank with a word that makes sense. Afterwards, you may compare your language with that of the author.

"Natalie," my mouth tries to say, but my throat is closed up tight. No sound comes out. I _____ [1] down, my arms flying helter-skelter, the shale _____ [2].

She has to be here. Maybe she's _____ [3] scouting for more stones. That's it. I _____ [4] down by the small rocky beach. A _____ [5] scuttles out from under a rock. Men _____ [6] a nearby ferry are laughing; the sound _____ [7] eerily loud though the boat is far _____ [8]. She isn't there. Over by the red _____ [9] bushes. No. Back by the greenhouse. No. _____ [10] way do I go?

I stop and _____ [11]. A voice . . . sounds. Behind me.

I spin _____ [12] run toward the voice. "Natalie?" I crash _____ [13] thicket. And then I see her. Natalie _____ [14] on a rock with someone. A man. _____ [15] is wearing a denim shirt and denim _____ [16]. A con. Natalie is sitting with a _____ [17].

The scream is stuck in my throat, _____ [18] me. Don't look away. Don't blink. Do _____ [19] blink.

The con is smiling. He's missing _____ [20] front tooth. There are dark greased comb _____ [21] in his hair. I wonder about this. _____ [22] aren't allowed hair pomade. Suddenly this seems _____ [23] important. Why is he wearing pomade on _____ [24] hair? Maybe he isn't a con. Please, _____, [25] don't let him be a con.

I _____ [26] even looked at Natalie. I'm afraid to _____ [27] my eyes off the guy in the _____ [28] shirt. I think somehow I can protect _____ [29] this way. But now I watch her _____. [30] She's smiling. Sometimes Nat looks concerned or _____, [31] or raging mad. The best she ever _____ [32] is interested. But here is my sister, Natalie Flanagan, looking happy.

POST-READING ACTIVITIES

1. Return to the Anticipation Guide in the Pre-Reading Activities on page six of this study guide. Fill in the "Author" column by placing a check [✔] next to each column with which the author would agree. Compare your responses with those of your classmates. Discuss those statements in which your responses did not agree with those of the author.

2. Return to the K-W-L chart that you began on page five in the Pre-Reading Activities. Based on the knowledge you have gained, correct any errors and add new information to column three. Then compare your chart with those of your classmates.

3. Return to the character chart that you began on page thirteen of this study guide. Complete the chart and compare your responses with some of your classmates. Select one of Moose's characteristics and describe how he exhibited this trait throughout the novel.

4. Return to the conflict chart on page sixteen of this study guide. Are there any additional conflicts to add? Have all conflicts been resolved? If not, how do you think they might be resolved?

5. Many famous criminals were imprisoned at Alcatraz besides Al Capone. Do some research to learn about some other inmates of Alcatraz, such as Machine Gun Kelly, Roy Gardner, and Robert Franklin Stroud. Then make up prisoner information cards as Theresa does for Al Capone. Share these cards with your classmates.

6. Imagine that you are interviewing the members of the Flanagan family for a television show about living with an autistic child. Write the dialogue. Plan the questions you will ask and the characters' responses. With classmates playing the parts of the characters, tape the interview to play for the class.

7. **Cooperative Learning Activity:** Work with a group of your classmates to find one or more passages in the book that convey a strong message. Present these passages to the other groups in your class and tell why they have been selected. Compare your selections with those chosen by other groups. Were there any passages that were chosen by more than one group?

8. Imagine that this story is told from another point of view. Rewrite a chapter or episode from the point of view of Mrs. Flanagan, Mr. Flanagan, Piper, or Theresa. Exchange your rewrite with a partner. As you read each other's work, notice how the story has changed.

9. Pretend that five years have gone by since the end of the novel. Write a short sequel to *Al Capone Does My Shirts*, telling what has happened in the lives of the major characters.

Post-Reading Questions and Activities (cont.)

10. **Readers Theater:** Read a chapter of the book as though it were a play. Choose a chapter that has a lot of dialogue and has two or more characters in conversation. Select a classmate to read each role and then select another to read the narration. The characters should read only those words inside the quotation marks. Ignore phrases such as "he said" or "she said." You may want to use simple props, such as hats, to identify the characters or small objects to identify the setting.

11. **Literature Circle:** Have a literature circle discussion in which you tell your personal reactions to *Al Capone Does My Shirts*. Here are some questions and sentence starters to help your literature circle begin a discussion.
    - How are you like Moose? How are you different?
    - Did you find the characters in the novel realistic? Why or why not?
    - Which character did you like the most? The least?
    - Who else would you like to read this novel? Why?
    - What questions would you like to ask the author about the novel?
    - It was not fair when . . .
    - I would have liked to see . . .
    - It didn't understand . . .
    - I wonder . . .
    - Moose learned that . . .

SUGGESTIONS FOR FURTHER READING

Fiction

Ayres, Katherine. *Macaroni Boy*. Yearling.

* Boyne, John. *The Boy in the Striped Pajamas*. David Fickling Books.

* Byars, Betsy. *Summer of the Swans*. Puffin.

* Curtis, Christopher Paul. *Bud, Not Buddy*. Yearling.

Draper, Cynthia. *Out of My Ming*. Athenieum.

* Giff, Patricia Reilly. *Pictures of Hollis Woods*. Yearling.

Hale, Marion. *The Truth About Sparrows*. Square Fish.

* Holt, Kimberly Willis. *My Louisiana Sky*. Square Fish.

* Hunt, Irene. *No Promises in the Wind*. Berkley.

* Lord, Cynthia. *Rules*. Scholastic.

* Mullaly, Lynda. *Fish in a Tree*. Puffin.

Ogaz, Nancy. *Buster and the Amazing Daisy: Adventures with Asperger Syndrome*. Jessica Kingsley Publishers.

_____. *Wishing on the Midnight Star: My Asperger Brother*. Jessica Kingsley Publishers.

* Paterson, Katherine. *The Great Gilly Hopkins*. HarperCollins.

Rodowsky, Colby. *Clay*. HarperCollins.

* Shyer, Marlene Fanta. *Welcome Home, Jellybean*. Aladdin.

* Yep, Laurence. *Dragonwings*. HarperCollins.

Zinnen, Linda. *Holding at Third*. Puffin.

Nonfiction

Braun, Eric, *Escape from Alcatraz*. Capstone.

Greenspan, Stanley, M.D. *The Child With Special Needs*. Perseus Books.

Murphy, Claire Rudolf. *Children of Alcatraz: Growing Up on the Rock*. Walker.

Stacey, Patricia. *The Boy Who Loved Windows*. Da Capo Books.

Thumann, Anna. *Alcatraz Schoolgirl*. CreateSpace.

Other Books by Gennifer Choldenko

Al Capone Shines My Shoes. Puffin.

Chasing Secrets. Yearling.

If a Tree Falls at Lunch Period. HMH Books.

No Passengers Beyond This Point. Puffin.

Notes From a Liar and Her Dog. Penguin.

* NOVEL-TIES study guides are available for these titles.

ANSWER KEY

Chapters 1 – 5
Vocabulary: 1. d 2. f 3. b 4. e 5. a 6. h 7. c 8. g; 1. asylum 2. compartments 3. humane 4. affliction 5. convicted 6. obedient 7. tantrums 8. evasion

Questions: 1. The Flanagan family comes to live on Alcatraz Island so that Natalie can attend the Esther P. Marinoff School where children with special needs are educated. 2. On his first night on Alcatraz, Moose sleeps with his clothes on and a baseball bat under the covers. He does this because he is nervous about living on the site of a prison with convicts all around him. 3. Mrs. Flanagan celebrates Natalie's tenth birthday annually so that she will seem to be younger than Moose, and her lack of cognitive development will be less evident. 4. Piper comes to the Flanagans' house to satisfy her curiosity about the new family, and she insists on taking Moose and Natalie on a tour of the island. 5. Moose is angered by Piper at their first meeting because she is insensitive to Natalie's feelings and is bossy. 6. Natalie shoes how important Moose is in her life when she cries the one time Moose does not ask if the sun got up okay; on the way to San Francisco, he is the only one who can get her off the boat by reading index pages with her; and once off the boat in San Francisco, she clings to him. 7. After the family leaves Natalie at the school, Moose feels guilty and is worried that his sister will be unhappy there.

Chapters 6 – 10
Vocabulary: 1. e 2. d 3. h 4. g 5. c 6. b 7. a 8. f; 1. remedial 2. hordes 3. radiant 4. heinous 5. sarcastic 6. incredibly 7. deliberately 8. contraption

Questions: 1. The warden calls Moose into his office in order to assert his authority and acquaint him with the five rules to follow while living on Alcatraz. He also requires Moose to help his daughter Piper with her school projects. 2. The warden does not want to invite media attention to the island by discussing the inmate Al Capone or life on Alcatraz. 3. Moose feels self-conscious because he is a stranger in his classroom, knowing only Piper, whom he considers an enemy. He worries about the first impression he is making. 4. In Miss Bimp's class, Piper breaks Rule #4 by talking about Al Capone in the outline for her oral report. 5. When Piper gives her outline, she says that Moose can back up her stories about Alcatraz. Since he does not want to anger her, he changes his outline to do so. 6. Moose is reluctant to help Piper in her scheme to sell the Alcatraz laundry service to kids at school because it means breaking one of the warden's rules and he mistrusts Piper and the nature of the scheme itself. 7. When Moose makes a double play in a baseball game, the other boys respect him and he feels part of their group. Then, when he is on the island, he becomes friendly with Annie when she shows her skill in throwing and catching a baseball. 8. The children manage to get balls from the convicts' game when they come over the prison yard wall from the recreation yard. 9. Annie tells Moose to get along with Piper or he will put his father's job at risk. 10. Mr. Purdy calls the Flanagans to tell them that Natalie cannot remain at the school.

Chapters 11 – 15
Vocabulary: Across–1. unresponsive 4. facility 6. mercilessly 8. adjustment 10. natters 12. revving 13. miraculously; Down–2. residential 3. replicate 4. frustrating 5. diagnosis 7. cultivated 9. wheedle 10. notorious 11. skirmish

Questions: 1. When she receives the news that Natalie must leave school, Mrs. Flanagan first seems lifeless, but later becomes angry. 2. Moose is proud of his mother for pressuring Mr. Purdy to give her the name of someone who might help Natalie, but he is angry that she will automatically do whatever he advises. 3. Mr. Purdy feels Natalie is not ready for his school because she was screaming for her buttons early in the morning, disturbing the people living in the houses surrounding the school. 4. Moose finally agrees to help Piper with her laundry project in exchange for Piper's vow that she will be kind to Natalie. 5. Moose's plan to play baseball on Mondays is ruined when his mother tells him he must watch Natalie so she can give piano lessons. Her solution to the problem is to have Moose ask Scout if baseball can be moved to Tuesdays. 6. Moose gets Natalie to put on her blue dress by letting her take her buttons outside and promising to take her swimming later. 7. Moose is happy that Natalie is with him when they go to watch the convicts march because he uses her as an excuse to Piper, the reason why he does not want to get an even closer view of the convicts.

Chapters 16 – 20

Vocabulary: 1. elaborate   2. preposterous   3. indignity   4. shenanigans   5. unseemly   6. culpability
7. quavering   8. procuring

Questions: 1. Piper's customers are disappointed because they expected some sign that convicts did the laundry, such as blood or bullet holes; instead, they just receive clean clothes. 2. Having shifted Monday baseball to Tuesday on Moose's account, Scout becomes angry at Moose once he learns that he will not be able to play on Tuesday, after all: his mother now must give piano lessons on Tuesday, instead of Monday. 3. Being able to divide in her head, Natalie helps the children by telling just how much each child should receive and handing out the money. 4. The warden found out about Piper's laundry project through an irate letter written by Del's mother. 5. When the other children tell the warden that the laundry project was Piper's idea, he looks very upset and his hands shake. Then he says he cannot trust any of the children and they will all be punished. 6. Natalie becomes quiet and rigid after Moose accidentally upsets her intricate grid of buttons, rocks, and feathers. 7. Moose is surprised by the degree of his father's anger because in the past he had always been patient with his son and rarely meted out punishment.

Chapters 21 – 26

Vocabulary: 1. offense–something that causes anger or hurt feelings   2. possessive–showing a strong desire for owning things or controlling people   3. humiliation–shame   4. pace–rate of walking   5. eroded–wore away   6. verge–at the point where something begins or happens   7. diligent–doing one's work in a careful, steady way   8. helter-skelter–in disorderly haste

Questions: 1. Since her fit the day the children met with the warden, Natalie has not had any fits and has been easier to deal with. 2. Piper wants the children to be on the specific boat because Al Capone's mother is coming to Alcatraz, scheduled on that boat. 3. Against Piper's wishes, Theresa brings her baby brother Rocky on the boat on Sunday. 4. Piper tries to get Mrs. Capone's attention by dropping her purse on the woman's toe. This doesn't work because Mrs. Capone ignores her, giving all her attention to a letter. 5. Mrs. Capone is captivated by Rocky, who is crying. She rocks him and sings him a song until he falls asleep. 6. Mrs. Capone does not get to visit her son because her corset sets off the metal detector. After she is strip-searched, she leaves because the humiliation is too much for her to bear. 7. Moose and Scout become friends again when Miss Bimp pairs them together for a journalism project and they do not refer to their former grievances. 8. Moose is happy about Natalie's imitation of Mrs. Kelly because it shows a level of understanding that Natalie has never exhibited before. 9. When Moose finds Natalie in conversation with convict 105, it becomes clear that Natalie had not been referring to 105 birds, but to the same convict that she had talked to on another occasion.

Chapters 27 – 32

Vocabulary: 1. e   2. c   3. g   4. a   5. b   6. f   7. d; 1. forlorn   2. hover   3. selective   4. jeopardize   5. strapping   6. repel   7. disloyal

Questions: 1. Moose is rough with Natalie because he is upset and afraid about what might have happened with convict 105. 2. Moose, who is still upset from his encounter with convict 105, slams the door in Natalie's face because she wants to find out how he acquired the baseball. When Natalie provides the number 105, Piper insists on knowing what this means. 3. Piper is excited about Natalie's relationship with convict 105 because she sees this as a way to begin another "business venture," such as getting Al Capone's signature and selling it. 4. Moose confronts his mother about Natalie's age because he realizes that denying his sister's true age might actually put her in danger. 5. Moose's mother, unaware of the real problem with convict 105, and convinced that Natalie will be accepted at the Marinoff School if her schedule at home is not changed, is furious that her son no longer takes Natalie out of the house, as though this will impede her progress. 6. To force Moose to take Natalie outside, his mother takes Natalie's buttons with her and leaves only a piece of lemon cake. The result is that Natalie has a terrible tantrum. 7. Using the pronoun *I*, Natalie communicates, "I want to go outside." This is such a breakthrough for her that Moose feels he cannot deny the request. 8. Moose asks his father whether he is responsible for Natalie's behavior because he remembers him saying that she got worse when she was three, the year he was born. Mr. Flanagan tries to assure his son that he is not the cause of his sister's condition.

Chapters 33 – 36

Vocabulary: 1. obsessed 2. attitude 3. vulnerable 4. obnoxious 5. teetering 6. rotation 7. understatement 8. seething

Questions: 1. Since Natalie's birthday comes one day before her interview at the Marinoff School, Mrs. Flanagan worries about how a birthday celebration and any change in schedule might adversely affect her daughter's chances of having a successful interview. 2. Mrs. Flanagan chooses not to stay home the day before the interview because she thinks Moose is better with Natalie than she is. 3. According to Piper, she drops by the Flanagan's apartment to wish Natalie a happy birthday. 4. Natalie uncharacteristically forges ahead so that she can go to the place where she always meets convict 105. 5. As Moose watches Natalie with 105, he is upset that she is holding hands with a convict, but happy that she is doing something normal for a sixteen-year-old girl. 6. Moose wants his mother to face reality and admit what is obvious to everyone else, even Mr. Purdy, that Natalie is sixteen. 7. Mrs. Flanagan tells Moose that she is no longer angry with him because she realizes that Moose expressed his thoughts about Natalie's age because he thought it would help Natalie. 8. As the person whose apartment is closest to the telephone, Mrs. Caconi comes to the Flanagan's apartment because she needs to tell the family the result of Natalie's interview.

Chapters 37 – 40

Vocabulary: 1. c 2. a 3. d 4. c 5. a 6. b 7. b 8. d

Questions: 1. Realizing that Carrie Kelly is the only one who has made some improvement in Natalie's life, Moose calls to thank her and ask her if the Esther P. Marinoff School would really help his sister. 2. The warden refuses Moose's request that he solicit Al Capone's aid in getting Natalie into school because he does not want to show preferential treatment to Al Capone or even bend the rules to ask anything of the gangster. 3. Mrs. Flanagan calls in sick for work and stays in her room all day in her bathrobe. Natalie becomes sullen because she thinks her mother is angry with her for not being accepted. 4. Piper helps Moose by telling him how to write the letter so that it will look like it has already been censored. Then she sneaks it into a pile of already censored letters. 5. Moose is greeted by his sister, the warden, and his parents who share with him the good news that the school has accepted Natalie as the first student in their school for older children. 6. It is strange that Mr. Purdy failed to mention opening a new branch of the school at Natalie's interview.